Days That Changed the World

D-DAY

Colin Hynson

Gareth Stevens
Publishing

Please visit our web site at: www.garethstevens.com
For a free color catalog describing our list of high-quality books,
call 1-800-542-2595 (USA) or 1-800-387-3178 (Canada).
Our fax: 1-877-542-2596.

Library of Congress Cataloging-in-Publication Data
Hynson, Colin.
    D-Day / by Colin Hynson.
      p. cm. — (Days that changed the world)
      Summary: Describes the Allied landing on the beaches of Normandy on June 6, 1944,
with an overview of events leading to that invasion as well as a description of its momentous
effects on the war.
      Includes bibliographical references and index.
      ISBN-13: 978-0-8368-5568-5   ISBN-10: 0-8368-5568-X (lib. bdg.)
      ISBN-13: 978-0-8368-5575-3   ISBN-10: 0-8368-5575-2 (softcover)
      1. World War, 1939–1945—Campaigns—France—Normandy—Juvenile literature.
[1. World War, 1939–1945—Campaigns—France—Normandy.] I. Title. II. Series.
D756.5.N6H93   2004
940.54'2142—dc22   2003060557

This North American edition first published in 2004 by
World Almanac® Library
An Imprint of Gareth Stevens Publishing
1 Reader's Digest Rd.
Pleasantville, NY 10570-7000 USA

This U.S. edition copyright © 2004 by World Almanac® Library. Original edition copyright © 2003 by ticktock
Entertainment Ltd. First published in Great Britain in 2003 by ticktock Media Ltd., Unit 2, Orchard Business
Centre, North Farm Road, Tunbridge Wells, Kent TN2 3XF. Additional end matter copyright © 2004 by
World Almanac® Library.

We would like to thank: Tall Tree Ltd, Lizzy Bacon, and Ed Simkins for their assistance.

World Almanac® Library editor: Carol Ryback
World Almanac® Library cover design: Steve Schraenkler

Photo Credits:
t=top, b=bottom, c=center, l=left, r=right, OFC=outside front cover
Alamy: 1, 7b, 8-9, 10, 12, 16-17, 18, 30t, 30-31, 42tl, 42b. Album Archive: 14-15, 42tr.
CORBIS: 7t, 10-11, 19, 25t, 27t, 30bl, 32, 33, 34t, 35t, 36-37, 37bl, 38t, 38-39, 41, 43br.
Hulton Archive: 4-5, 20-21, 23c, 24t, 25, 26-27, 28t, 29b.

Printed in the United States of America

2 3 4 5 6 7 8 9 10 09 08

CONTENTS

In the early morning hours of June 6, 1944, a huge invasion fleet set sail across the English Channel. From ports across the southern coast of England, about 5,000 ships carried more than 200,000 soldiers over a dull, gray sea. Neither the soldiers nor the officers knew their destination. All they knew was that this day was called "D-Day."

U. S. General Dwight D. Eisenhower often greeted his troops.

Europe faced a terrible threat in the 1930s, when Hitler's Nazi party swept to power in Germany. As Germany rearmed itself and expanded its territory by invading the Rhineland, and soon afterward invaded Czechoslovakia and Austria, the world stood by in fear. But on September 1, 1939, when the Nazis marched into Poland, Britain and France declared war on Germany. World War II had begun.

Soldiers used some ferocious-looking weapons in vicious, hand-to-hand fighting.

In the early days of the war, Hitler's troops seemed almost unstoppable. Then in 1941, the United States entered the war when Japan bombed Pearl Harbor, Hawaii. Up until that point, the Allied Forces had achieved a series of victories over Germany, but Hitler's troops still controlled much of Europe.

The liberation of Nazi-occupied Europe finally began with the great sea invasion of France known as D-Day. The Allies defeated the mighty German army, freed Western Europe, and helped bring an end to World War II.

Hitler's refusal to withdraw troops helped the Allies win World War II.

Strategic placement of rubber tanks helped make the Germans believe that troops were massing in Southern England and preparing to invade Pas de Calais, France.

INTRODUCTION

Thousands of U.S. servicemen who died on D-Day and in the battles for the surrounding territory afterwards lie in the Normandy American Cemetery overlooking Omaha Beach.

Hitler's army spent four years building its defenses against a coastal invasion. The Germans expected Allied Forces to attempt a landing along the northern French coast, but they were not certain exactly where or when it would begin.

The Allied fleet formed an impressive armada on D-Day. More than five thousand transport and warships and thousands of fighter and bomber aircraft were marshalled to protect the invading Allied forces from the fierce German resistance they expected to encounter.

The Allied D-Day invasion took German Field Marshal Erwin Rommel and his troops by surprise.

Soon after each ship left port, its officer opened a sealed envelope containing detailed instructions and maps. Their destination: the north coast of France, also called Normandy. Bombers sent in advance of the armada attacked German defenses, and twenty thousand paratroopers landed to secure Normandy's main roads and bridges. Despite the armada's size, every Allied soldier expected a bloody fight on the beaches of Normandy.

Both sides paid a heavy price for the D-Day landings. More than 2,500 Allied soldiers died and about 10,000 were injured. By best estimates, the Germans suffered similar casualties.

The success of the D-Day landings helped shape the Europe we know today. Yet few of the troops waiting to land that morning thought of

Europe's future. As the thud and rumble of battle grew louder, their only thought was whether or not they would still be alive at day's end.

Europe is now a far safer place, and a peaceful Germany lies at the heart of Europe. France and Germany use the single European currency, the Euro, and plans exist for a European Army.

But every June sixth, people gather to honor those who so many years ago gave up their lives so that others could be free and live in peace.

Today, Germany lies at the political heart of Europe. It holds a seat at the European Parliament (above) and uses the single European currency (the Euro).

Britain's prime minister, Winston Churchill, was a source of great inspiration to the people of Britain — and beyond — during World War II.

The reason for the war in Europe and for D-Day can be traced back to the end of World War I in 1918. In the aftermath of defeat, anarchy, and economic depression, many Europeans rejected democracy and turned to dictators for the answers to their problems. The actions of two of these dictators — Adolf Hitler in Germany and Benito Mussolini in Italy — set all of Europe on a course for another world war.

The Nazis organized mass rallies at Nuremberg, a city in southern Germany. These spectacular demonstrations of Nazi power were carefully stage-managed and calculated to arouse people's fanaticism in support of the Nazi Party. Flags, marching, and music were all highly ritualized. Hitler's speeches climaxed the rallies.

The Treaty of Versailles

World War I, which claimed the lives of more than twenty million people, finally ended in 1918. The following year, the Treaty of Versailles set up the punishment for Germany, the aggressor in World War I. After four years of war, Germany was forced to scrap most of its armed forces and to give up land to neighboring countries. It also began to pay crippling sums of money to Britain and France for war damages. This treaty caused a great deal of resentment in Germany.

The Rise of the Nazis

Political and economic chaos reigned in postwar Germany. High inflation made currency worthless and unemployment soared. People blamed the democratic government for the worsening situation and turned to extremist parties for solutions. Adolf Hitler's Nazi Party received more votes in each election as the number of unemployed grew. In 1930, the Nazis won 6.5 million votes. In 1932 — the worst year of the Great Depression — the Nazis received more than 13 million votes and became the largest party in the German coalition government. When Hitler became the chancellor of Germany in 1933, he also became one of the most powerful men in Europe.

THE GREAT *Depression*

Between 1929 and 1935, the world's economies endured the Great Depression. This enormous economic slump caused businesses all over the world to close and millions of people lost their jobs. Germany was especially hard hit, with more than six million people unemployed. Rocketing inflation also wiped out the value of people's savings, causing widespread poverty.

Fascism in Italy

Italian fascism was born in March 1919 when Benito Mussolini founded the *Fascio di Combattimento*, an anti-socialist fighting force. Mussolini believed that Italy should become a great power and dreamed of building a new Roman Empire. His Fascists formed armed groups to terrorize political opponents. In October 1922, the Fascists set out to take over the government by force in their "March on Rome." Mussolini's new dictatorship was an inspiration to the Nazis, and the Italian leader allied himself with Hitler throughout the war.

Germany rearms

Hitler's first task upon becoming chancellor was to begin rearming Germany, even though the Treaty of Versailles specifically forbade it. In 1935, Hitler reintroduced conscription. The German army grew from 100,000 in 1933 to about 500,000 by 1936. The German navy and air force also expanded.

Hitler's beliefs

Hitler combined an extreme German nationalism with a belief in the supremacy of the Aryan "race." He planned to acquire land for his "master race" through the military conquest of the "inferior" Slavic peoples.

In 1935, the swastika, an ancient religious symbol, became the official emblem of the Third Reich — the Nazi Party's name for Hitler's regime.

ADOLF Hitler

Adolf Hitler was born in Austria in 1889. As a young man, he lived in Vienna, where he earned a meager living painting watercolors. When World War I broke out in 1914, he joined the German army and served as a corporal. Feeling betrayed by Germany's defeat, Hitler joined the small organization called the German Workers' Party and transformed it into the Nazi Party. In 1924, he was jailed for trying to overthrow the Bavarian government. His book, *Mein Kampf* (My struggle), outlined his vision for a new Germany.

Hitler and his ally, Mussolini (left) met frequently. The Nazis borrowed many ideas and symbols from Italian fascism.

Hundreds of small civilian boats raced across the English Channel in May 1940 to help evacuate the British army from the beach at Dunkirk, France, before the Germans arrived.

DEFEAT *at Dunkirk*

As the German spearhead thrust deeper into France, the British army gathered on the French coast at Dunkirk, where it awaited evacuation to Britain. From May 27, 1940 to June 4, 1940, more than 200,000 British and 140,000 French troops reached England by crossing the English Channel in an incredible assortment of yachts, tugs, trawlers, ferries, and fishing boats. The troops left behind all their tanks and heavy guns. Germans seized most of Britain's best equipment intact.

Had Britain and France sent troops to the Rhineland, Hitler would almost certainly have backed down and perhaps even abandoned his plans for territorial expansion. Their failure to act only encouraged Hitler to continue.

The end of Austria

Hitler's next aim was to create a "Greater Germany" by uniting Germany and Austria. Austrian Nazis paved the way by destabilizing their country with riots and bombings. In March 1938, Hitler threatened to send in troops "to restore order." Faced with such aggression, the Austrian chancellor resigned and his Nazi replacement welcomed Hitler's troops. Many people in Austria supported Hitler. The country was renamed "Ostmark" and became a province of Germany.

In the meantime, however, Hitler wanted to eliminate the people he thought were undermining Germany: communists, liberals, and, most of all, the Jews — whom he blamed for Germany's defeat in World War I and for the humiliation of the Treaty of Versailles. Hitler deprived Jews of all rights and later killed millions of them.

Germany's first move

The Treaty of Versailles forbade the German army from going within about 3 miles (50 kilometers) of the Rhine River. But in March 1936, Hitler sent 32,000 troops into the Rhineland and in doing so risked starting a war with France and Britain. However, France and Britain did nothing at that time. The British did not feel that the presence of German troops in the Rhineland posed a threat. This assumption proved disastrous for Europe.

Czechoslovakia falls

Hitler used similar tactics in the Sudetenland, an area on the borders of Czechoslovakia that was home to three million ethnic Germans. In October 1938, Germany occupied the Sudetenland to "protect" the Sudeten Germans. Hitler promised Britain that this was his final territorial demand in Europe. Then, in early April 1939, his army marched into the rest of Czechoslovakia, absorbing half of it into Germany and installing a puppet ruler (someone whose actions are controlled by another) to govern the rest. Only then did Britain and France wake up to the danger facing Europe.

War begins

Too late, Britain and France realized that Hitler was not about to stop at the borders of Czechoslovakia. Soon, their worst fears were confirmed. Hitler set his eyes on the "Polish Corridor," an area of Poland that Germany lost after World War I. Britain and France agreed to protect Poland if it was attacked. They also believed that the neighboring Soviet Union would never tolerate a German-occupied Poland. To the world's astonishment, Hitler pulled off a major diplomatic coup. In August 1939, he signed the Nazi–Soviet Nonaggression Pact with the Soviet Union, the Nazis' greatest ideological enemy, in which both sides agreed not to fight each other and to carve up Poland between them. On September 1, 1939, German forces invaded Poland. Two days later, Britain and France honored their promise to Poland and declared war on Germany. Soviet forces later attacked Poland on September 17, 1939. Poland was divided between the Soviet Union and Germany.

France surrenders

French and British forces were too far away to help Poland. During the first few months of the war,

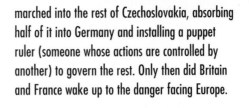

The rapid advance of the German troops forced thousands of people, including this little girl (center), to flee their homes. Refugees clogged roads and slowed the retreat of British and French forces.

Thanks to the tactic of blitzkrieg (lightning war), Germans became nearly invincible during the early stages of World War II. German forces paraded through almost every European capital.

BLITZKRIEG

The German army enjoyed its early successes thanks to a new tactic called *blitzkrieg* (lightning war). Blitzkrieg involved launching a sudden, fast-moving attack with tanks, fighter planes, and bombers, designed to take an enemy completely by surprise.

there was little fighting. This period is often called the "Phony War." In spring 1940, German forces occupied four other countries: Denmark, Norway, Belgium, and Holland. Next, they invaded France, defeating the French army in a rapid blitzkrieg offensive and forcing the British army to withdraw. The French surrendered without fighting a single major battle.

The Battle of Britain

Britain now stood alone. Hitler knew that in order to invade Britain he first had to control Britain's skies. This meant knocking out the Royal Air Force. On August 8, 1940, the German air force — the "Luftwaffe" — began attacking airfields in southern England. The Luftwaffe had twice as many aircraft as the British and were confident of an easy victory. After fierce fighting during the last two weeks of August, the Royal Air Force (RAF) had lost most of its best pilots and was close to defeat. Yet in September, Hitler suddenly ordered his planes to stop attacking airfields and instead begin a bombing campaign against British cities.

The RAF used this vital lull to recover and regain control of Britain's skies.

The Blitz

The intensive German bombing of British cities, particularly London, is known as "the Blitz." Hitler believed the Blitz would force Britain to negotiate or surrender. The Blitz caused massive devastation. It killed more than 30,000 people, damaged or destroyed more than three million homes, and flattened several city centers. German bombing continued from September 1940 until May 1941, when Hitler decided to turn his attention eastwards toward his next invasion target: the Soviet Union.

Britain hits back

The British refused to let the Blitz defeat them. In the autumn of 1940, RAF bombers attacked Germany, and, during the winter, bombed Berlin. Unfortunately, the British lost many planes and the bombing caused minimal effect on German industry and morale.

Battle of the Atlantic

With Europe now in Nazi hands, Britain imported supplies from the United States and Canada. German submarines, known as U-boats, attacked and sank far more supply ships than the British could replace. Britain might have been starved into submission. The pause in the Blitz, however, meant

For many years, Winston Churchill (below) was among the few British politicians who warned about Hitler. Nobody listened. When Churchill became prime minister in 1940, he promised that Britain would fight and never surrender.

CHURCHILL *speaks*

Winston Churchill maintained British morale during the darkest days of the war with his stirring speeches. In June 1940, just after the evacuation of Dunkirk, Churchill ended a speech with, "Let us therefore address ourselves to our duty and so bear ourselves that if the British Commonwealth of Nations and Empire lasts for a thousand years, men will say, 'This was their finest hour.'"

that British planes could protect ships, which now traveled in convoys for safety. German U-boats remained a problem, but Britain managed to import its supplies anyway.

A picture taken during the Blitz (left), shows St. Paul's Cathedral between the smoke and flames of bomb-damaged London streets.

North Africa

Britain's oil supplies traveled from the Middle East through Egypt's Suez Canal and through the Straits of Gibraltar in the Mediterranean Sea. Italian troops attacked British forces stationed in Egypt to protect the oil shipments but were beaten back. However, the Germans came to the aid of their Axis allies. In 1941, General Erwin Rommel (known as the "Desert Fox") and his troops pushed British and Commonwealth troops almost to the Suez Canal.

Operation Barbarossa

Hitler had always dreamed of a German empire in the East, and had already planned an invasion of the Soviet Union. Soviet leader Joseph Stalin did not believe that Hitler would ever invade. On June 22, 1941, the Germans launched Operation Barbarossa, an attack on the Soviet Union. It took the Soviet army completely by surprise. Hitler's tanks rolled rapidly across the Ukraine in what seemed like an easy German victory.

Dad's Army, a very popular television series and movie, celebrated the British Home Guard.

At last! Their epic story invades the Big Screen!

DAD'S ARMY

COLUMBIA PICTURES PRESENTS
DAD'S ARMY ARTHUR LOWE · JOHN LE MESURIER · CLIVE DUNN
A COLUMBIA PRODUCTION
JOHN LAURIE · JAMES BECK · ARNOLD RIDLEY · IAN LAVENDER · LIZ FRASER
SCREENPLAY BY JIMMY PERRY AND DAVID CROFT · PRODUCED BY JOHN R. SLOAN
DIRECTED BY NORMAN COHEN TECHNICOLOR [C]
General Exhibition

DAD's *army*

The British expected a German invasion at any time during the dark days of 1940 and 1941. They called upon civilians to defend the country. More than 250,000 men joined what became known as the Home Guard. Since most of these men were too old to fight in the regular armed forces, many people called them the "Dad's Army."

PRELUDE TO WAR

German advances

The Germans staged a spectacular advance into the Soviet Union. Within months, Hitler's armies captured nearly three million prisoners of war and destroyed most of the Soviet air force. The Soviet army was already severely weakened: most of its best generals were killed in the 1930s on Stalin's orders. Between June and December 1941, the Soviet Union lost more than four million men and nearly all of the country's food supplies. By the winter of 1941, the Germans troops reached the outskirts of Leningrad and Moscow.

War in the Far East

For the people of China and Japan, World War II began in 1931. Japan attacked and occupied a large area of China known as Manchuria in a bid to gain land and valuable resources such as oil. In 1937, Japanese troops invaded the rest of China, and in 1941 attacked other Asian countries. Soon Japanese forces threatened the Philippine archipelago and India. Fierce Japanese fighters seemed almost unstoppable.

The Japanese attack on Pearl Harbor (right) changed the U.S. viewpoint regarding the war in Europe. The United States quickly realized it was their war, too.

TOO *late*

Many believed that the Japanese attacked Pearl Harbor without first declaring war on the United States. In fact, the Japanese ordered their ambassador in Washington, D.C., to deliver a message declaring war before the attack. However, the coded message was so long that by the time the ambassador deciphered and delivered it, the attack had already started.

Pearl Harbor, Hawaii

The Japanese believed that to gain control of Asia and the Pacific Ocean they had to destroy the U.S. Navy. Three hundred sixty Japanese aircraft attacked the U.S. Pacific Fleet at Pearl Harbor, Hawaii, at 8:00 A.M. on December 7, 1941. By 10:00 A.M., the attack was over, leaving nearly 2,500 dead and fourteen U.S. ships destroyed. President Franklin D. Roosevelt asked Congress to declare war on Japan on December 8, 1941.

JOSEPH *Stalin*

Between 1929 and 1953, Joseph Stalin ruled the Soviet Union. A secretive, paranoid, and ruthless dictator, Stalin showed no mercy for rivals. Millions died or were sent to labor camps during the "Great Terror" of the mid-1930s. Stalin fatally weakened his army when he purged it of thousands of officers.

Soviet leader Stalin (left), came to power in 1929 following Lenin's death. His name means "man of steel" in Russian.

By mid-1942, the German and Japanese armies appeared invincible. Hitler had conquered most of Western Europe, and the Soviet Union teetered on the point of collapse. Japan controlled Hong Kong and Singapore, and its forces swarmed all over southeast Asia and the Pacific Ocean islands. Yet by year's end, the Allies had halted both the German and Japanese advances and slowly began pushing them back.

1942: Red areas highlight the territory controlled by Germany and Italy; Japan controlled the blue areas.

JUN/4/42 In June 1942, U.S. forces inflicted a major defeat on the Japanese navy at the Battle of Midway in the Pacific Ocean. As an armada of 185 Japanese ships advanced toward the Midway Islands, squadrons of U.S. bombers launched from three aircraft carriers to meet the threat. The battle was conducted entirely by planes; U.S. and Japanese ships never actually exchanged fire.

The Japanese lost nine important ships, including three aircraft carriers, within two days.

OCT/23/42 In North Africa, German troops under General Rommel had attacked the British in June, capturing the stronghold of Tobruk, Libya, in the Western Desert. Then the British retreated and waited. They were commanded by General Bernard Montgomery, a cautious strategist, who waited until he built up his forces before launching a decisive attack at El Alamein, Egypt, on October 23, 1942. The following month, U.S. and British troops landed in Algeria. The Germans and Italians were now fighting on two African fronts.

A German tank grinds to a halt on the Soviet steppes. The environment was a major factor in Hitler's Soviet campaign. Engines clogged with dust in summer and froze in winter. Nesting rodents sometimes ate the tanks' wiring!

Three U.S. planes return from a mission at Guadalcanal. U.S. air power helped remove the Japanese from this strategically important island in the Pacific Ocean.

FIELD MARSHAL *Rommel*

Field Marshal Erwin Rommel was one of Germany's most famous soldiers. He commanded German troops in North Africa and set up the defense of France against the Allied invasion. In October 1944, Rommel committed suicide after being implicated in plot that failed to kill Hitler in July 1944.

JAN/3/43 After months of bitter fighting, Japanese troops began their withdrawal from the strategic Pacific island of Guadalcanal (one of the Solomon Islands east of New Guinea). By February 1943, the Japanese completed their evacuation of Guadalcanal.

FEB/3/43 By the summer of 1942, German troops reached the southern Soviet city of Stalingrad. As the city that bore Stalin's name, its fate was very symbolic for both sides. Hitler was determined to capture it; Stalin was determined to defend the city whatever the cost. German troops soon became mired in ferocious street fighting, but Hitler refused to allow a retreat. As winter approached, the Soviets sprang an enormous trap, encircling the Germans and cutting off their supplies. On February 3, 1943, the remains of Hitler's army, starving and frozen, surrendered. It was the Germans' first major defeat and marked a turning point of the war for the Soviets.

MAY/13/43 After the Allies' decisive victory of El Alamein in October 1942, the British pushed Rommel's *Afrika Korps* across Libya to Tunisia, where on May 13, 1943, 250,000 German and Italian troops surrendered.

MAY/22/43 During the spring of 1943, the Battle of the Atlantic reached a climax when German U-boats sank twenty-seven ships bringing supplies from the U.S. to Britain. However, by this time British codebreakers had secretly cracked the Germans' "Enigma" cipher (code). The Allies could now read coded German messages and discover the U-boats' positions. In May 1943, Allied bombers inflicted such heavy losses on the U-boats that the Germans withdrew their fleet.

JUN/10/43 In June 1943, the Allies coordinated their strategy for bombing targets in Germany, beginning a campaign of around-the-clock raids. The British bombed at night and the U.S. by day. This wore down German morale and disrupted Hitler's war economy.

DWIGHT D. Eisenhower

Known to everybody as "Ike," Dwight D. Eisenhower was born in 1890 in Texas. He attended military school and worked his way up through the ranks. Ike displayed great talent as an organizer and had a reputation as someone who liked to involve everyone when making his plans, rather than just ordering people around.

Dwight D. Eisenhower (center) commanded U.S. forces in Europe while Bernard Montgomery (third from right) headed the British units. Eisenhower and "Monty" seldom agreed on strategic approaches.

"Like pulling a piece of spaghetti across a plate, rather than trying to push it."

General Eisenhower describes his own style of leadership

"Ike and I were poles apart."

General Montgomery discusses his U.S. counterpart

JUL/5/43 After the disaster at Stalingrad, Hitler regrouped his armies and finally decided to take the Soviet city of Kursk. On July 5, 1943, he attacked with an army of 1,000,000 men and 2,700 tanks. Hitler's hesitations gave the Soviets time to prepare. The German army's defeat was so great that it never again launched a major offensive in the East.

JUL/10/43 With North Africa now cleared of Hitler's forces, the Allies used Tunisia as a springboard for the invasion of Italy. On July 10, 1943, Allied troops landed on the Italian island of Sicily, capturing it within a month. On July 25, Mussolini was overthrown, and the new government indicated that it wanted to negotiate a surrender with the Allies. By September, the British had landed on the Italian mainland, but Hitler reacted swiftly by invading Italy, and rescued his friend Mussolini in a daring commando raid.

AUG/43 In August 1943, U.S. and British military leaders met to discuss strategy. Throughout 1943, the Allied leaders argued among themselves about the best way forward. The U.S. joined the war because of the actions of the Japanese, but they agreed that the Nazi menace in Europe must be tackled first. The Soviets pressured the Allies to open a second front against the Germans in Western Europe; slogans such as "Second Front Now" began to appear on walls and bridges in Britain. British support for an offensive grew. But Roosevelt and Churchill could not agree on when or where to stage the invasion of Europe. U.S. commanders pushed for an early offensive; the British remained much more cautious because of a number of defeats in Europe, including the raid on Dieppe, France in 1942. They preferred to concentrate on defeating the Germans in North Africa and Italy.

DIEPPE *the failed invasion*

One of the reasons for British caution over D-Day was the disastrous failure of an earlier Allied attack on Dieppe, France. During that August 1942 raid, six thousand soldiers — mostly Canadians — landed in Dieppe. The Germans mustered their forces to beat back the invaders, killing or capturing about half of all the Allied troops that participated.

NOV/28/43 In November 1943, the "Big Three" Allied leaders — Franklin D. Roosevelt, Winston Churchill, and Joseph Stalin — met in Tehran, the capital of Iran. Stalin and Roosevelt argued for an invasion of France as soon as possible. Churchill reluctantly found himself out-voted. They set the invasion date for May 1944 on the beaches of Normandy, along the northern coast of France. Roosevelt appointed General Dwight D. Eisenhower as overall commander of the invasion. British General Bernard Montgomery would command ground forces after the invasion.

Eisenhower and Montgomery came from very different backgrounds and disagreed on many things, particularly matters of military strategy.

JAN/44 By January 1944, about two million U.S. and Canadian troops had arrived in England. The British called this massive influx of troops the "Friendly Invasion." The presence of the mostly young, foreign troops had a huge impact on the daily lives of the British people. Many people — particularly young British women — welcomed the U.S. soldiers. However, U.S. and British rivalries often caused fights between troops.

The "Big Three" — (left to right) Stalin, Roosevelt, and Churchill — met in November 1943 at the Tehran Conference in Iran to plan the Allied invasion of Europe. Stalin was at first very suspicious of his two allies. He suspected them of delaying a second front in the West so that Germany and the Soviet Union would exhaust themselves fighting — resulting in a weakened Germany and the collapse of communism in the Soviet Union.

> "Towards the end of 1943, our backwater, which British soldiers had garrisoned so sparsely for four years, overflowed almost overnight with GIs. How different they looked from our own jumble-sale champions, beautifully clothed in smooth khaki, as fine in cut and quality as a British officer's — an American private, we confided to each other at school, was paid as much as a British captain, major, colonel."

Historian John Keegan reminisces about the arrival of U.S. soldiers in England when he was a boy.

INVADING *Norway*

A series of false radio messages broadcast from Scotland tricked the Germans into believing that the Allies planned to attack occupied Norway. As a result, the Germans kept many troops and supplies in Norway.

APR/27/44 U.S. troops used Slapton Sands Beach in Devon, southwest England, to rehearse boarding and disembarking from amphibious landing craft. Local village people were relocated in order to keep the rehearsals secret. On April 27, 1944, German ships attacked vessels

Troops move a rubber tank into position. The Allies' deception operation aimed to fool the Germans into thinking an army was massing in southeast England — with the purpose of invading France by crossing the Straits of Dover and landing at Pas de Calais.

GI *brides*

U.S. ("GI") servicemen were very popular with British women and many romances occurred between them. By the end of the war, more than 80,000 British women had married U.S soldiers and left their homes to live in the United States.

carrying U.S. troops to Slapton Sands. Nearly seven hundred Americans were killed. Tensions ran high among the men training on the English beaches. Every soldier — no matter what country he was from — knew that he was preparing and training for the invasion of Europe, and that whenever the call came, he had to be ready for it.

MAY/44 Preparations for the invasion intensified in absolute secrecy throughout May 1944. One of the reasons the Dieppe raid failed in August 1942 was that the Germans learned when and where the landing would take place. This time, the Allies went to elaborate lengths to ensure that the Germans would not discover their plans. In the months prior to the invasion, the Allies launched "Operation Bodyguard," an ingenious plan to prevent the enemy from guessing the time and place of D-Day. Deliberate Allied leaks of false information made the Germans suspect that a huge army in southeast England was preparing to invade France at Pas de Calais, the French port nearest to Britain. To make the ruse convincing, the Allies built fake camps and inflated rubber tanks, which the Germans spotted from the air. Meanwhile, the real invasion army secretly prepared in southwest England. Alongside the soldiers, paratroopers also trained for their parachute drops into France. By late May, every serviceman and woman knew that D-Day loomed.

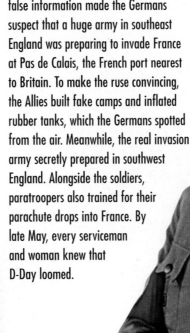

Although many British men resented the presence of Allied troops in their country, thousands of British women fell in love with and married U.S. soldiers.

The Allies knew it was crucial to keep the Germans guessing about where and when a coastal invasion would happen. If Hitler's forces had discovered the time and place of D-Day, the operation would have had a low chance for success.

OPERATION OVERLORD

I n May 1944, Allied forces agreed on a date and time for the invasion of Normandy. D-Day was set for June 5, and the time, called H-Hour, was 6:00 A.M. U.S., British, and Canadian forces were assigned different landing beaches. The commanders stopped all mail service from U.S. forces to the United States and cut the transatlantic telephone lines in order to maintain secrecy. Soldiers stationed at ports from where the invasion would begin were forbidden to leave their bases. On June 4, the Allies faced bad weather and rough seas in the English Channel. They had no choice but to delay the invasion until June 6, when forecasters predicted a temporary break in the weather.

THE INVASION BEGINS  00:00

What became known as "The Longest Day" began in darkness as 13,000 paratroopers jumped from planes into the Normandy invasion area. Their mission was to seize bridges and help protect the main landing force. Soon afterwards, nearly 2,000 Allied bombers attacked German positions further inland. Members of the French Resistance helped by destroying telephone lines. By 6:00 A.M., an approaching armada of more than 5,000 ships became visible from the Normandy coast. Guns from Allied ships began shelling German defenses on the beaches.

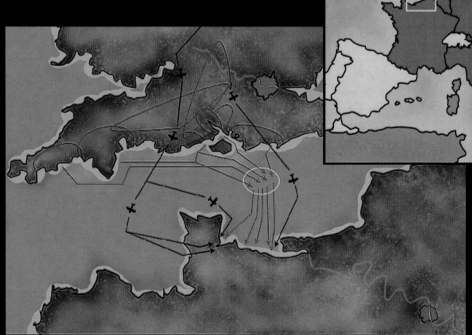

The square box on this map of Europe shows the invasion site. Allied territory is blue, Axis territory is red, and neutral countries are yellow.

Ships carrying Allied ground forces left England, joined up at the area indicated by the yellow circle, and sailed to the five Normandy beaches marked by red arrows.

VIEWPOINT

"I saw in the first breaking light of dawn the outline of our escort destroyer close on our starboard side. My sickness and misery was suddenly added to by shock and dismay [by] an explosion that lifted the destroyer out of the water amidships."

— Briton "sapper" Alfred Lane describes the Gold Beach landing

"Before embarking we were told there would be 10,000 Allied planes attacking today and there is every sign our air mastery is complete. So far, not a single German plane has been seen."

— Sir Charles Birkin, remarking on the Allied air supremacy

"In the absence of orders, go find something and kill it."

— Field Marshall Erwin Rommel who was surprised by the Allied invasion of France

OMAHA BEACH — 06:00

U.S. troops landed at the beaches code-named Omaha and Utah. Omaha Beach was about 5 km (3 miles) long. Nearly two-thirds of the entire U.S. force — about 45,000 troops — landed on this short stretch of sand. Earlier Allied bombing had failed to knock out the German defenses lining the beach bluffs. As the U.S. troops landed, they waded through the surf amid showers of German bullets. Machine guns trained on the beach below killed many U.S. soldiers the instant they landed. To make the situation even more desperate, so many landing craft crowded the beach that they could hardly maneuver and became easy targets for the Germans. Meanwhile, a Ranger unit ("Colonel Rudder's Rangers") scrambled up a sheer cliff about 100 feet (30 m) high to destroy what turned out to be a decoy German gun battery at Pointe du Hoc. At least two thousand Americans lost their lives on "Bloody Omaha" Beach on D-Day.

UTAH BEACH — 06:30

U.S. troops landing at Utah Beach, the westernmost Normandy beach, experienced a much different situation from those of their comrades at Omaha Beach. Landing troops met little resistance from the Germans stationed at Utah Beach. Once U.S. troops crossed the beach, however, they found themselves wading through flooded fields. Overall, about two hundred U.S. servicemen died taking Utah Beach on D-Day.

07:00 GOLD BEACH — 07:00

British troops landed at the beaches code-named Gold and Sword. Earlier Allied air raids failed to damage German bunkers at Gold Beach as much as hoped, and, as a result, a hail of machine-gun fire greeted the British landing parties. Most of the men killed at Gold Beach died within the first few minutes of landing there.

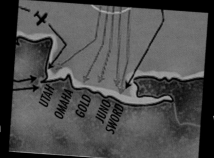

OPERATION OVERLORD

JUNO BEACH `07:45`

Canadian troops landed at Juno Beach between the British targets of Gold and Sword Beaches. They arrived at 7:45 A.M., fifteen minutes late. By that time, the rising tide covered more of the beach, leaving a smaller landing area available to the troops. Again, the landing parties suffered high casualties during the first few minutes of arrival.

Canadian forces stream onto the shore of Juno Beach. (above, and right; upper and lower)

SWORD BEACH `09:00`

Special tanks that could explode hidden mines aided the troops landing at Sword. By 10:30 A.M., Sword Beach had been cleared of German defenses. Within two hours, some British troops advanced more than half a mile (1 km) inland from Sword Beach.

British troops landing at Sword Beach faced little resistance.

OMAHA BEACH

 09:15

The U.S. troops landing at Omaha Beach faced brutal resistance. General Omar Bradley, commander of the Omaha landing, came close to ordering a retreat. The troops desperately needed special Sherman tanks — called DD (Duplex Drive) tanks — to help them break through the strong German defenses. Inflatable canvas devices on the DD tanks enabled them to float, and two propellers pushed them through the water. Unfortunately, rough seas swamped most of the tanks and many of them simply sank far from the shoreline with their crews inside.

General Omar Bradley led the Omaha landing.

VIEWPOINT

"When the boat hit the shore and the ramp went down everybody did supposedly what they had to do. The riflemen were fanning out but the casualty rate was very bad. We couldn't determine where the firing was coming from because there was something like one hundred yards of open beach ahead of us and all we could see were the houses along the shoreline. I can remember dropping into the sand and taking up my rifle and firing it at one of the houses. Sergeant Wilkes said to me, 'What are you firing at?' I said, 'I don't know. I don't know what I'm firing at.'"

— Private George Roach, a 19-year-old U.S. soldier who landed at Omaha Beach

OMAHA BEACH

 10:30

The soldiers at Omaha slowly crawled up the beach trying to find shelter from the bullets flying at them. Some of the troops managed to reach the top of the beach bluffs and attack the Germans. Within a few hours, U.S. forces had broken the German defenses and taken control of a road. U.S. troops began to move inland — but at a high price. Casualties numbered at least 2,500 killed or wounded; more than 1,000 died the moment they landed.

After landing at Omaha Beach, U.S. soldiers faced fierce attacks from German troops.

OPERATION OVERLORD

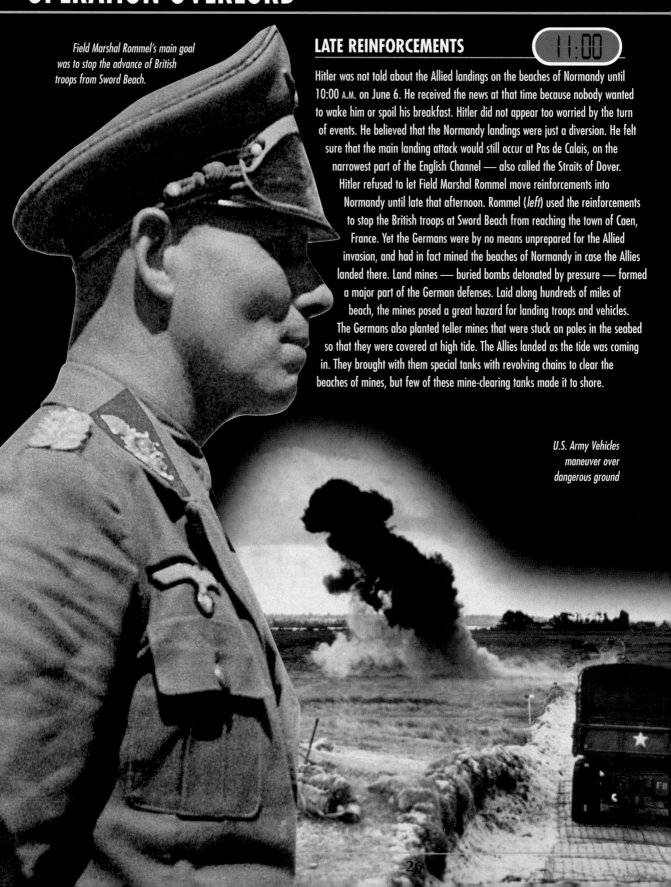

Field Marshal Rommel's main goal was to stop the advance of British troops from Sword Beach.

LATE REINFORCEMENTS

`11:00`

Hitler was not told about the Allied landings on the beaches of Normandy until 10:00 A.M. on June 6. He received the news at that time because nobody wanted to wake him or spoil his breakfast. Hitler did not appear too worried by the turn of events. He believed that the Normandy landings were just a diversion. He felt sure that the main landing attack would still occur at Pas de Calais, on the narrowest part of the English Channel — also called the Straits of Dover. Hitler refused to let Field Marshal Rommel move reinforcements into Normandy until late that afternoon. Rommel (*left*) used the reinforcements to stop the British troops at Sword Beach from reaching the town of Caen, France. Yet the Germans were by no means unprepared for the Allied invasion, and had in fact mined the beaches of Normandy in case the Allies landed there. Land mines — buried bombs detonated by pressure — formed a major part of the German defenses. Laid along hundreds of miles of beach, the mines posed a great hazard for landing troops and vehicles. The Germans also planted teller mines that were stuck on poles in the seabed so that they were covered at high tide. The Allies landed as the tide was coming in. They brought with them special tanks with revolving chains to clear the beaches of mines, but few of these mine-clearing tanks made it to shore.

U.S. Army Vehicles maneuver over dangerous ground

VIEWPOINT

"I waited patiently all night for some instructions. But not a single order was received by me. I finally decided, at 6:30 in the morning, that I had to take some action. I ordered my tanks to attack the English Sixth Airborne Division."

— Edgar Feuchtinger, commander of a division of German tanks, explains his frustration at the lack of action by German leaders.

"The assignment was a new one for the German Wehrmacht (Armed Forces), since, up to this point, they had not spent much thought on seaborne landings and defenses against such landings."

— Admiral Friedrich Ruge, naval adviser to Erwin Rommel

ROMMEL'S PROBLEMS `16:00`

Rommel found it very difficult to coordinate the German response to the invasion. A weakened Luftwaffe presented little challenge to the landing troops. Allied paratroopers and bombers and the French Resistance shattered the Germans' lines of communication and disrupted the railroad tracks. Surprisingly, even Rommel expected a second invasion elsewhere and did not bring in troops from Pas de Calais. Within a few days of D-Day, Rommel realized he could not drive the Allies back across the Channel; all he could do was retreat beyond the range of Allied guns. Hitler was furious and German casualties mounted.

A CLOSE CALL `23:00`

The biggest risk faced by the Allies on D-Day was getting trapped on the beaches and being slaughtered by the Luftwaffe and German reinforcements. If the Germans had coordinated their response more effectively, or if Hitler had given his order sooner, the Germans might have overpowered the Allied landings. But within twenty-four hours of D-Day, the Germans lost their chance forever. Hitler's "Atlantic Wall" — a line of concrete coastal defenses — was in Allied hands.

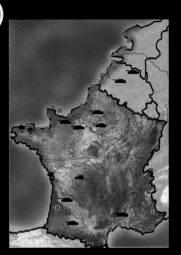

Under the supervision of Allied forces, Nazi soldiers captured on D-Day carry a wounded soldier to an aid station.

By the end of D-Day, Allies held all the coastal defenses (shown in red).

OPERATION OVERLORD

MAKING A HARBOR

JUN 6

One problem faced by the Allied planners was that by June, 1944, the Germans controlled all the harbors in Normandy. Without the use of a natural harbor where big ships could dock and unload, the Allied D-Day invasion would end at the beaches. While this did not matter all that much on D-Day, it became crucial afterwards as troops moved inland. Long before D-Day, the Allies realized they would have to build two artificial, floating harbors to deliver men, food, and equipment — but how? The solution: They built huge concrete blocks formed in England and towed them across the Channel. Like giant Legos, the blocks fit together to create long piers, code-named "Mulberries," off the Normandy Coast. The Mulberries played a vital role in delivering the 28,000 tons (26,000 tonnes) of supplies needed during the weeks after D-Day. Storms destroyed the U.S. Mulberry by mid-June.

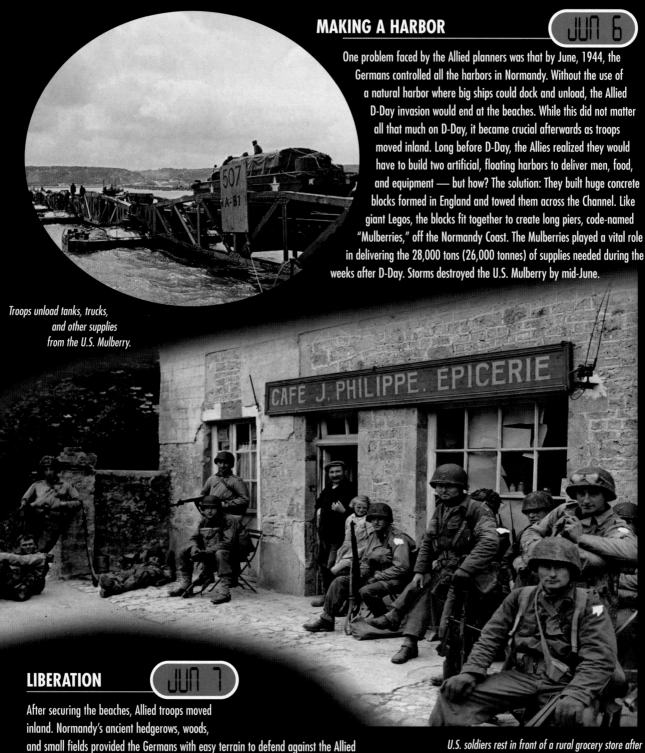

Troops unload tanks, trucks, and other supplies from the U.S. Mulberry.

LIBERATION

JUN 7

After securing the beaches, Allied troops moved inland. Normandy's ancient hedgerows, woods, and small fields provided the Germans with easy terrain to defend against the Allied attackers. Nevertheless, within a day of the landings, the Allies advanced through the French countryside. U.S. paratroopers liberated St. Mere Eglise on D-Day. U.S. ground forces officially liberated their first town, Bayeux, in northern France on June 7, 1944.

U.S. soldiers rest in front of a rural grocery store after advancing inland from their D-Day invasion of Normandy, France. A French citizen smiles from the doorway.

VIEWPOINT

Barrage balloons floating overhead offer protection against German strafing airplanes as troops join up and unload supplies at Juno Beach.

JOINING UP — JUN 8

In order for the Allies to secure the beaches, the different armies on each landing beach had to create an unbroken line of Allied troops. Otherwise, the Germans might push through any gaps and keep the Allies separated. U.S. troops from Omaha Beach linked with British troops from Gold Beach on June 7, 1944. The next day, Canadian units from Juno Beach joined up with the English troops at Sword Beach. Finally, on June 10, 1944, U.S. troops from Utah and Omaha Beaches met to form that vital continuous line.

CAEN — 10:6:44

The Allies hoped to take Caen, a city of 50,000 people, as quickly as possible. Beyond Caen lay the road to Paris, and, eventually, Germany. If the Allies controlled Caen, the war would end sooner. Rommel knew this, too, and was determined to prevent the Allies from taking Caen. He brought in his best battle-hardened troops who had already fought against the Allies in the Soviet Union and Italy. Ferocious German resistance at Caen slowed the Allied advance. The Allies could not move forward, and the Germans could not push them back.

OPERATION OVERLORD

HE STORM JUN 19

thin two weeks, bad weather — and not German oops — threatened the Allied advance from the ast. On the night of June 19, 1944, the biggest orm in nearly a century in the English Channel used convoys of supply ships to turn back. The orm lasted for three days. Wind and high aves damaged the U.S. Mulberry beyond pair. Allied troops could do nothing but wait til the bad weather passed. The storm owed the Allies' planned advance by veral important days. However, even fore the storm damage was repaired, 00,000 more Allied troops stood ready to ght, their sites set on Cherbourg, a large ort town on the French mainland. With the pture of Cherbourg and its harbor and rport, the Allies could use larger ships and rcraft for faster delivery of men and supplies.

Young people of Cherbourg eagerly await the arrival of Allied forces.

THE TAKING OF CHERBOURG JUN 28

The U.S. assault on Cherbourg began on June 22, 1944, with a massive bombardment and ended with the capture of the important port town six days later.

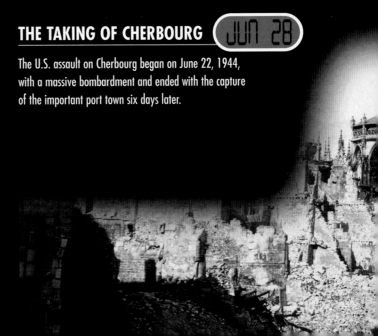

VIEWPOINT

THE BOMBING AND LIBERATION OF CAEN

JUL 9

British and Canadian forces began moving toward Caen on D-Day, but the Germans managed to hold the city for a month despite repeated Allied assaults. Finally, on July 7, 1944, four hundred fifty Allied bombers dropped thousands of tons of explosives on Caen. Two days later, on July 9, 1944, the Allies finally drove the Germans away and entered a city razed to the ground by the Allied bombardment.

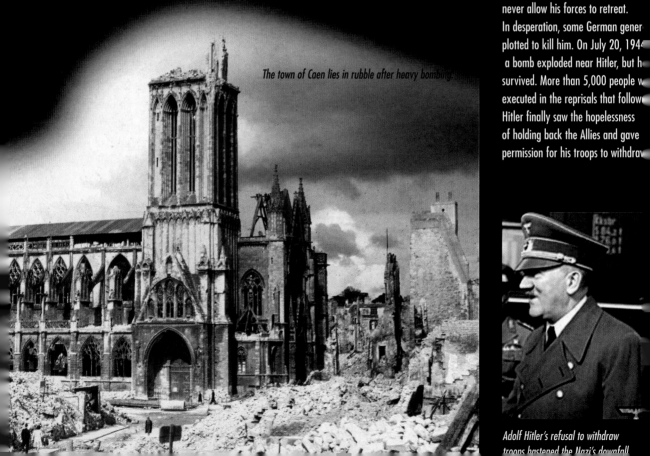

The town of Caen lies in rubble after heavy bombing.

ATTACK ON HITLER

JUL 2[

HItler himself was another reason the Allies made sure but slow progre across France. His commanders wan to withdraw and wait for the Allies t reach German lines, but Hitler woulc never allow his forces to retreat. In desperation, some German gener plotted to kill him. On July 20, 194 a bomb exploded near Hitler, but h survived. More than 5,000 people w executed in the reprisals that follow Hitler finally saw the hopelessness of holding back the Allies and gave permission for his troops to withdraw

Adolf Hitler's refusal to withdraw troops hastened the Nazi's downfall

PUSH TO VICTORY

Field Marshal Erwin Rommel, the "Desert Fox," committed suicide before war's end.

General Montgomery (left) shows Winston Churchill (center) plans for the Allied advance through Europe.

The Germans were now fighting the war on several fronts. As the Allies pushed forward from Normandy toward the borders of Germany, they also landed in southern France. In Italy, Allied troops advanced northward, while to the east, the Soviets were gaining ground. The Germans knew that victory was slipping away. Retreat was their only option.

Germany in retreat

Under Field Marshal Walther Model, the German army was in full retreat. More than 20,000 of his troops died in Normandy and 200,000 were taken prisoner. Model could not sustain such losses. Now he could only fight to slow the Allied advance rather than drive them back. By July 1944, Rommel's vow to throw the Allies "back into the sea" seemed a distant dream.

Paris liberated

The speed of the Allied advance sent shock waves throughout occupied Europe, electrifying the mood of the people and filling them with hope that liberation was finally at hand.

Eisenhower at first decided to move U.S. troops around Paris rather than to capture it. However, on August 19, as the Allies approached, French Resistance fighters rose up in revolt against the Germans. On August 25, U.S. forces liberated Paris. General Charles de Gaulle led French troops triumphantly down the Champs Elysées in a victory march to cheering crowds on August 26, 1944. By month's end, almost all of France was free again.

Belgium and Holland

With France mostly under Allied control, troops moved northward to face the Germans occupying Belgium and Holland. By September 4, British troops held the two most important cities in Belgium — Antwerp and Brussels. A new Soviet

PARIS *saved*

As the Allies moved rapidly toward Paris, and its citizens rose up against the Germans, Hitler gave orders to destroy Paris. Dietrich von Choltitz, the German governor of Paris, ignored this order and instead surrendered the city. Thanks to these actions, some of the most famous buildings in the world, including the Eiffel Tower and the Louvre art museum, survived the World War II.

CHARLES *de Gaulle*

General Charles de Gaulle guided the French Resistance during the German occupation. Roosevelt and Churchill disliked de Gaulle, but many French citizens considered him a hero. Although Paris would not have been freed without Allied help, de Gaulle insisted that French troops liberate Paris. After the war, de Gaulle served as President of the French Republic from to 1958 to 1969. He died of a heart attack in 1970.

The Free French army receives an ecstatic welcome as its tanks roll past the Arc de Triomphe (in background) and down the Champs Élysées in Paris (below).

> "The Americans and French were about to liberate Paris, so we drove there in a couple of jeeps. There was a lot of shooting going on when we arrived. We drove round to the Ritz. The Germans were going out of the back, as we drove up and booked in."
>
> *Major Peter Carrington (later Lord Carrington), one of the few British troops in Paris when it fell to the Allies in August 1944*

offensive in the east, which coincided with the campaign in Normandy, forced the Germans to divide their fighting between fronts and helped the Allies gain territory.

A bridge too far

In September 1944, the British believed that if they captured three bridges over the Rhine River, they would move into Germany more quickly. Paratroop drops were planned to take the bridges, with ground troops racing in to meet them. This plan worked for the first two bridges, but at the furthest bridge — at Arnhem in Holland —

the paratroopers met very heavy resistance and the ground troops could not reach them. After eight days of fighting, the British retreated. Only 2,500 of the 10,000 troops that landed escaped.

Stopping for the winter

As the winter of 1944 closed in, the Allies slowed their advance. Their commanders understood the difficulties of fighting in cold, wet weather. Allied troops had moved so far so quickly by then that delivering fresh supplies, food, and ammunition presented a problem. The Soviet army faced the same shortages caused by their rapid advance.

> *"Starvation has reduced their bodies to skeletons. The fact is that all these were once clean-living and sane and certainly not the type to do harm to the Nazis. They are Jews and are dying now at the rate of 300 a day … they are too far gone to be brought back to life."*
>
> British soldier Peter Combs wrote a letter home after witnessing the liberation of Belsen concentration camp in April 1945

DEATH *camps*

As the Allies advanced into Germany, they made a horrifying discovery. The Nazis ran hundreds of labor and extermination camps where they "eliminated" Jews, Gypsies, and other groups. About fourteen million people died in these camps. Six million of them were Jews.

The last offensive

In December 1944, the Germans launched a daring attack on Allied troops in a part of Belgium known as the Ardennes. The attack — called the "Battle of the Bulge" by U.S. forces, took the Allies completely by surprise. They had not expected an attack during the winter. At first, the German offensive was very successful. They used some extra-large, 70-ton (63 tonne) "Royal Tiger" tanks and quickly created a bulge in the area of land held by U.S. troops. But soon the Nazi tanks ran out of fuel. The Allies began their counterattack. The Germans' last major attack outside Germany turned into a victory for the Allies.

"Miracle" weapons

Even as late as June 1944, Hitler still thought he could win the war with the aid of his new "miracle" weapons. The Germans developed two types of "vengeance" missiles — the V-1 and V-2 — using new rocket technology. V-1 missiles made a distinct incoming sound, while the V-2 missiles struck targets in silence. More than a thousand of these missiles hit southern England, causing terror and panic. Once the Allies captured the rocket bases in northern Germany, the threat vanished.

In this famous photograph (right), Soviet troops raise the Soviet Union's flag over the Reichstag, the German parliament, in Berlin, Germany, in April 1945.

The Soviet push

In early 1945, Churchill and Roosevelt asked Stalin to put more pressure on the Germans in the East in order to take some of the strain off the Allies. Stalin obliged with a massive offensive beginning on January 12, 1945. Soviet forces swept through Poland and into Germany. They covered about 300 miles (480 km) in just 18 days, coming to within 40 miles (65 km) of Berlin.

The bombing of Dresden

In the west, U.S., Canadian, and British troops advanced slowly. To help them, Allied commanders launched a new bombing campaign against German cities. U.S. bombers targeted factories. British bombers tried to break German morale by smashing the cities. On February 13 to 14, 1945, Allies bombed the city of Dresden.

On May 7, 1945, General Alfred Jodl signed the unconditional surrender of all German forces to the Allies.

The Allied bombing killed more than 25,000 German civilians. This remains one of the most controversial Allied actions of the war.

Surrender

Stalin wanted the Soviets — not the Allies — to capture Berlin. In mid-April, Soviet troops began their attack. The tiny, shattered German army, comprising mainly of old men and young boys, faced a Soviet force of two million, armed with 6,000 tanks and 5,000 aircraft. The outcome was inevitable. On April 30, Hitler shot himself. Berlin surrendered the next day. The rest of Germany's forces officially surrendered on V-E Day, May 8, 1945. The war in Europe was over.

The end of the war

After the victory in Europe, World War II continued for another four months in the Pacific Theater. In the end, deadly new technology decided the outcome of the war when the U.S. dropped atomic bombs on the Japanese cities of Hiroshima and Nagasaki in August 1945. Japan's official surrender on September 2, 1945 brought to an end years of destructive fighting. Now it was time to build the peace.

> "I saw a couple of V-2s being launched somewhere in the north across the Maas [River], which was still in German occupation. These horrible lethal missiles were making their lethal ascent. I presumed they were destined for London ... and my heart trembled."
>
> Brigadier Tony Wingfield on witnessing a V-2 rocket pass overhead in 1944

After the war, Europe was divided into two opposing camps: one led by the United States and the other by the Soviet Union. This division affected the lives of Europeans in many ways. It decided what kind of country they lived in, what their jobs were, and where they could travel. But by the end of the 1980s, the political climate was changing again and a new Europe began to emerge.

World War II redefined Europe (map, above). The European continent was divided into East and West, and into NATO countries and Warsaw Pact countries.

The future of Europe

When the victorious Allies marched into a defeated Germany, they already had a postwar plan for Germany and the rest of Europe. In February 1945, Roosevelt, Churchill, and Stalin met at the Yalta Conference in present-day Ukraine to discuss how the Allies would divide and govern Germany after the end of the war.

Safe from Germany

Stalin's main concern was that Germany never again attack the Soviet Union, as it had done twice in thirty years. One way to ensure this was to turn the Soviet Union's neighboring European countries — Poland, Czechoslovakia, Hungary, Romania, and Bulgaria — into "buffer states." Each of those countries would have governments installed by the Soviets. Stalin made certain that only people he trusted became leaders of these new communist countries.

HARRY S Truman

Franklin D. Roosevelt died in April 1945, just about a month before the end of the war in Europe. Harry S Truman succeeded him as President of the United States. Truman feared the spread of Soviet influence in the world and, unlike Roosevelt, did not trust Stalin. This lack of trust contributed to the start of the Cold War — a state of tension and hostility between East and West. Without any actual fighting, the Cold War lasted for more than forty years.

Controlling Germany

The Allies decided to govern parts of Germany until they were sure it could be trusted to govern itself without threatening other countries in Europe. Despite the fact that Germany's capital, Berlin, was in the middle of Soviet-controlled territory, the Allies divided it into East and West Berlin.

Clash of ideals

Germany's occupation led to a split among the Allies. Huge ideological differences existed in the way the Western allies and the Soviet Union governed themselves. Western countries preferred democratic governments and free-market economies. The Soviet Union's single-party, state-based communism, did not allow free elections or a free market. During the war, these differences had been set aside, but by 1946, they were straining relations.

MARSHALL *plan*

The Americans helped Western Europe financially after the war with a program called "The Marshall Plan." The Plan allowed countries ravaged and bankrupted by war to rebuild their economies; it also ensured that none of these countries turned communist. The Soviet Union refused to allow countries under its control to receive any benefits from the Marshall Plan.

New military alliances

In 1948, the Soviets tried and failed to drive the other Allies out of Berlin. The following year, the United States and the British helped form the North Atlantic Treaty Organization (NATO), a military alliance opposed to the Soviet Union. The Soviet Union responded in 1955 by forming the Warsaw Pact, a military alliance of countries close to it. Mistrust that developed between the two groups became known as the "Cold War." Europe split into a pro-American West, and a pro-Soviet Union, communistic East.

The Berlin Wall

In 1949, the Soviets declared that their portion of Germany would become a separate country known as the German Democratic Republic of East Germany. Many Germans living in this section of Germany tried to escape into West Germany, the area controlled by the U.S., Britain, and France. In August 1961, the Soviets and East Germans suddenly built a concrete wall through the city. The wall separated communist East Berlin from the democratic western half of the city, and prevented people from traveling to the West. The Berlin Wall became one of the most potent symbols of the Cold War.

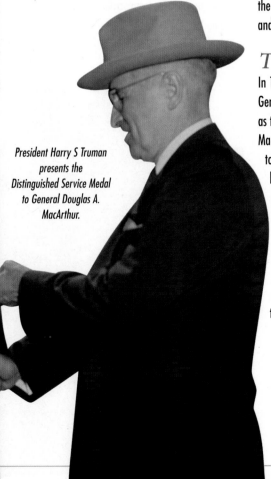

President Harry S Truman presents the Distinguished Service Medal to General Douglas A. MacArthur.

On August 13, 1961, East German forces suddenly sealed off the crossing points between East and West Berlin, and erected a barrier of concrete and barbed wire to prevent East Germans from moving to West Berlin.

EUROPE REDRAWN

The impressive European Parliament building is located in Brussels, Belgium.

A changed world

World leadership changed greatly after 1945. The United States, which was not a major world power before the war, emerged as an affluent superpower with enormous military might. In contrast, Britain's world-power status declined. Financially crippled after the war, the British Empire was breaking up at a rapid rate.

European Union

Along with NATO, another important organization emerged in Europe. In 1957, European governments signed the Treaty of Rome and formed the EEC (European Economic Community), known today as the European Union (EU). The EU has a European Parliament. Citizens cast their votes for what is in effect an international Parliament, the first of its kind in the world.

Soviet Union Changes

By then, many of the old communist leaders, some of whom had taken part in the Russian Revolution of 1917, had died. No one knew what kind of leader would succeed them. In 1985, Mikhail Gorbachev became head of the Soviet Union. He wanted to steer the country toward a more open and democratic government. Gorbachev introduced sweeping reforms that helped bring about the breakup of the old Soviet Union. Most of all, Gorbachev wanted an end to the Cold War, and before long, tension between the East and West began to diminish. Gorbachev's reforms also freed some countries from Soviet control. In 1989, realizing that the police would not stop them, the people of Berlin tore down the notorious Berlin Wall that had divided

JOSIP *Tito*

After World War II, the various states of Yugoslavia united under a communist government led by Josip Tito. In 1948, Stalin argued with Tito, whom he regarded as too liberal. From then on, Yugoslavia remained communist but did not take orders from the Soviet Union. Tito died in 1980. Ten years later, Yugoslavia broke up and the different states began to fight each other.

their city for nearly forty years. Less than a year later, in October 1990, Germany united into one country again, and most of the Warsaw Pact countries chose to become democracies. Then in 1991, the Soviet Union broke up, signifying the end of communism in Europe.

Russia's struggles

Gorbachev's successors did not fare as well, and the separate state of Russia lags behind other countries in Europe. Russian unemployment is high and many people are very poor. Other parts of the former Soviet Union, such as Chechnya, are fighting still for their independence. Widespread corruption and organized crime also make daily life in Russia difficult for ordinary citizens.

A NEW *Poland*

In 1980, the communist government of Poland permitted the existence of free trade unions. The popular unions soon became a political force, but were banned by the army the following year. By 1989, with change sweeping through the former Warsaw Pact countries, the main Polish union, Solidarity, was not only legal but also governed the country.

War in Yugoslavia

One war — in the southern European country of Yugoslavia — has occurred in Europe since the end of World War II. Yugoslavia, composed of various ethnic groups with different religions and cultures, became a communist country after World War II. When Yugoslavia's leader, President Tito, died in 1980, the country split into areas such as Serbia, Montenegro, and Croatia. From 1990 until 1996, war between parts of Yugoslavia continued.

In 2000, NATO took military action against Serbia, the dominant state of the former Yugoslavia, when it attempted to clear ethnic Albanians from the neighboring province of Kosovo. Serbia's attack caused an enormous humanitarian crisis.

*J*une 6, 1944 did more than simply bring World War II closer to an end — the events that followed D-Day helped shape modern Europe. The Normandy landings could have easily failed, causing a very different future not only for Europe, but also for the entire world. So many continue to remember D-Day and honor those who fought and those who sacrificed their lives for the liberation of Europe.

Thousands of servicemen who died on D-Day are buried in the American Cemetery overlooking Omaha Beach on the Normandy coast.

reunited to remember what is often called "The Longest Day." Posters everywhere said: "In June '44 we said 'Thank you.' In June '94 we say 'welcome.'"

June 1994

The 50th anniversary of the D-Day landings occurred in June 1994. All across Europe, people commemorated this important date, and prepared to celebrate the fiftieth anniversary of the end of World War II in 1995. In Normandy, many soldiers who fought on the beaches half a century earlier

British celebrations

British coastal towns from which troops sailed for Normandy in June 1944 team up with "sister" towns in Normandy to observe D-Day. In November each year in Britain, Remembrance Day is dedicated to honoring all British troops who served during World War II.

ROAD TO *Victory*

In 1998, the D-Day Museum in New Orleans, Louisiana, began a "Road to Victory," in which people could buy a brick engraved with the name of a D-Day veteran, and lay it at the museum. The D-Day Museum in Portsmouth, England, created the "Overlord Embroidery," which tells the story of D-Day. Based on the famous Bayeux Tapestry commissioned by William the Conqueror in the eleventh century, the Tapestry depicts the Battle of Hastings — the invasion of England from Normandy. The Overlord Embroidery shows the same journey between Normandy and England, but this time the ships sail in the opposite direction: south from England to liberate France.

U.S. celebrations

The United States became closely involved in the commemoration of D-Day. In 1994, President Bill Clinton traveled to Normandy and marked the fiftieth anniversary by addressing the veteran soldiers who had fought on D-Day.

Germans participate

After fifty years, much of the hatred and mistrust between German and Allied troops had disappeared. In a spirit of reconciliation, German veterans who had defended Normandy were invited to take part in the commemoration. For most of these old soldiers, the event marked a unique opportunity to recall their different experiences and to finally meet some of the men against whom they had fought on those beaches so very long ago.

The future

D-Day helped create a new Europe. Before June 6, 1944, most of Europe was either conquered by the Germans or ruled by dictators. After D-Day, Europe embarked on a new, peaceful chapter of its history. The strength of the European Union and of its single currency, the euro, demonstrate the way in which countries that were once enemies have worked together toward a common good. Over the next few years, many of the countries once under Soviet control may also join the European Union. This will help ensure that Europe's peace will continue to last.

A highly decorated D-Day veteran (left) from the United States participates in celebrations marking the fiftieth anniversary in June 1994.

VETERANS *commemorate*

In June 1994, the leaders of the countries that participated in D-Day commemorated the event on the beaches of Normandy. President Bill Clinton said, "We are the children of your sacrifice. We are the sons and daughters you saved from tyranny's reach." Clinton, born in 1946, was the first U.S. president born after World War II.

1918 – 1938

- November 1918: Germany's defeat in World War I leads to the signing of the Treaty of Versailles, which imposes harsh terms on Germany by Britain and France.

- January 1933: Adolf Hitler becomes chancellor of Germany and begins a program of rearmament and conscription in defiance of the Treaty of Versailles.

- March 1936: Hitler sends troops to reoccupy the Rhineland, an area of Germany demilitarized by the Treaty of Versailles.

- March 1938: Hitler invades Austria and incorporates it into the "Greater German Reich."

1938 – 1940

- October 1938: Hitler occupies the Sudetenland, a German-speaking area of Czechoslovakia, and promises Britain that it is his final territorial demand in Europe.

- March 1939: Hitler occupies the rest of Czechoslovakia unopposed.

- August 1939: Hitler signs a non-aggression pact with the Soviet Union to ensure that his invasion of Poland goes unopposed by the Soviets. The pact contains a secret agreement to divide Poland between Germany and the Soviets.

- September 1939: Britain and France declare war on Germany after Germany invades Poland on September 1, 1939.

- April–May 1940: Germany conquers Denmark, Norway, Holland, Luxembourg, and Belgium, and invades France.

- May 1940: Winston Churchill becomes prime minister of Britain.

1941 – 1942

- June 1941: Germany unleashes "Operation Barbarossa" — its invasion of the Soviet Union. Germans capture huge numbers of Soviet prisoners.

- December 1941: Japanese planes bomb the U.S. Pacific fleet at Pearl Harbor, Hawaii. The U.S. declares war on Japan. Germany declares war on the U.S.

- January 1942: the first U.S. troops arrive in Britain.

- June 1942: U.S forces inflict a major defeat on the Japanese at the Battle of Midway in the Pacific.

- August 1942: a landing raid by Canadian paratroops at Dieppe in northern France ends in disaster.

1942 – 1943

- October 1942: the British win a major victory against German forces led by Rommel at El Alamein in North Africa.

- February 1943: the German Sixth Army surrenders at Stalingrad, in the Soviet Union.

- May 1943: the Allies win the Battle of the Atlantic. Germany withdraws its U-boat fleet after heavy losses.

- June 1943: the Allies begin nonstop bombing raids on Germany.

- September 1943: British and American troops land in Italy. Germans troops invade Italy from the north.

1943 – 1944

- November 1943: the "Big three" — Roosevelt, Churchill, and Stalin — meet at the Tehran Conference and agree on a time and place for D-Day.

- January 1944: numerous military camps are built all over southern England in preparation for D-Day.

- June 1944: the invasion of Europe begins on the beaches of Normandy, northern France.

- July 1944: the Allies break out of Normandy after capturing the towns of Cherbourg and Caen. Nazi generals attempt an attack on Hitler, but fail to kill him.

- August 1944: Allied troops and the French Resistance liberate Paris. General Charles de Gaulle leads the victory march.

- December 1944: the Germans launch a final offensive known as the "Battle of the Bulge."

1945 – 1948

- February 1945: Allied bombing destroys Dresden, Germany. The Big Three meet at the Yalta Conference.

- April 1945: Soviet tanks enter Berlin; Hitler commits suicide.

- May 1945: Germany surrenders unconditionally to the Allies.

- July 1945: Berlin is divided between between a Soviet area of command and a Western area of command.

- August 1945: the United States drops atomic bombs on the Japanese cities of Hiroshima and Nagasaki, bringing an end to World War II.

- June 1948: the Soviets attempt to drive the United States, Britain, and France out of West Berlin by blockading the city. The United States and Britain fly in men and supplies. The Soviets back down rather than risk a war with the West.

1949 – 1961

- April 1949: NATO (the North Atlantic Treaty Organization) is formed. Western European states enter into a military alliance with the United States to provide each other with mutual military assistance in the event of an attack.

- May–October 1949: the Soviet-controlled area of Germany becomes the German Democratic Republic of East Germany, and the areas controlled by the U.S., Britain, and France become West Germany.

- May 1955: the Warsaw Pact is formed in which certain Eastern European states ally themselves with the Soviet Union in order to receive mutual military assistance in the event of an attack by NATO.

- March 1957: Treaty of Rome leads to the formation of the European Union (then known as the European Economic Community).

- August 1961: the Berlin Wall is erected to prevent people from leaving communist East Berlin for the freedom of West Berlin.

1962 – 1994

- March 1985: Mikhail Gorbachev becomes president of the Soviet Union and introduces wide-ranging reforms.

- 1989: the Berlin Wall is torn down after President Gorbachev indicates that the Soviet Union will not intervene militarily in Eastern Europe. The "Velvet Revolution" in Czechoslovakia and the "Christmas Revolution" in Romania, in which those countries' communist governments are overthrown, occurs. The Cold War ends.

- 1990: Germany reunifies after the communist government of East Germany collapses. The Soviet Union breaks up.

- 1992: the Maastricht Treaty is signed. It proposes a common foreign and security policy for all member states of the European Union.

- June 1994: Veterans celebrate the fiftieth anniversary of the Normandy landings.

aggression hostile, unprovoked attacks.

Allies the U.S., Britain, and other countries that fought against Nazi Germany, Italy, Japan, and their supporters during World War II.

amphibious military term for a vehicle that operates on land and sea. Amphibious landing craft landed in Normandy on D-Day.

armada large fleet of warships.

artillery large, heavy guns used for warfare on land.

Aryan an imagined "master race" of Nordic Caucasians.

atomic bomb a bomb that produces a massively destructive explosion through nuclear fission. World War II finally ended in the Pacific when the U.S. dropped atomic bombs on Hiroshima and Nagasaki, Japan, on August 6 and 9,1945, respectively.

Axis Nazi Germany, Italy, Japan, and any other countries allied with them during World War II.

Berlin Wall a barrier erected in 1961 to separate the Soviet-controlled area of East Berlin from the western area of the city controlled by the U.S., Britain, and France. It was torn down in 1989.

blitzkrieg (the Blitz) the German bombing of British cities — particularly London — by the Luftwaffe during World War II.

Bodyguard code name for the Allied operation to deceive the Germans into thinking that a large army was stationed in southeast England, and preparing for an invasion of Calais, France.

buffer state a smaller, less strategically or economically important country located between larger states that reduces the likelihood of hostility between the larger states.

communism a political system based on the notion that the government controls all property and everything is publicly owned.

conscription forced participation in a military organization.

DDs (Duplex Drive tanks) specially adapted amphibious Allied tanks that moved through water as well as over land.

D-Day June 6, 1944; code name for the date of the beginning of Operation Overlord, the Allied invasion of German-occupied Europe.

defensive position fighting on the side of the one under attack.

dictatorship a state in which all power rests in the hands of one individual, the dictator.

Enigma the German cipher machine used for encrypting military codes during World War II. In 1942, British code breakers secretly cracked it and could read German messages.

European Union an economic and political association of European countries founded in 1957 to promote free internal trade and a common identity while reducing the likelihood of another European war.

fascism an extreme nationalist, authoritarian political system, opposed to communism and democracy, usually characterized by a cult surrounding a charismatic leader and the crushing of opposition without regard for the law.

flank a military term for the right or left side of a body of troops.

free market an economy where prices and wages are determined by competition and demand.

French Resistance an underground organization of men and women who worked in secret to sabotage and disrupt the German occupation of France during World War II.

Friendly Invasion popular name for the mass influx of about two million U.S. and Canadian troops to Britain in the months prior to the Normandy landings of June 1944.

front a military term for the foremost line of battle or the foremost position of an army.

funnies a series of special tanks adapted by the Allies for various functions, such as mine sweeping, amphibious landings, flame-bridge-laying. The mine sweeper had a revolving drum attached to its front, from which steel chains exploded mines buried in the sand.

GI (government issue) a popular name for U.S. Army privates or anything related to the U.S. military

Gold code name for one of the Normandy beaches taken by British troops on D-Day.

H-Hour name for the hour of the commencement of an operation such as D-Day.

Juno code name for the Normandy beach taken by Canadian troops on D-Day.

land mines pressure-sensitive explosive devices buried just beneath the surface.

Luftwaffe the German air force during the war.

marshal to arrange troops or plans in a certain order.

Marshall Plan a U.S. plan to stimulate postwar European economic recovery through financial aid.

Mulberry one of two artificial harbors, used to unload men and supplies, built by the Allies after the invasion of Normandy.

NATO (North Atlantic Treaty Organization) an April 1949 treaty in which Western European states entered into a military alliance with the U.S. to provide each other with mutual military assistance in the event of an attack.

nazism an extreme form of fascism that preached the superiority of the German race and promoted anti-semitism.

offensive position fighting on the side of the attacker.

Omaha code name for a Normandy beach taken by U.S. troops during D-Day. Landing troops met with heavy machine-gun fire and suffered heavy losses, and the beach became jammed with damaged and abandoned equipment.

Overlord code name for the Allied invasion of Europe.

paratroopers troops trained to drop into areas by parachute.

RAF (Royal Air Force) the British air force.

rivals enemies.

sapper a military demolition expert.

Soviet Union (Union of Soviet Socialist Republics; USSR) a country formed from the territories of the former Russian empire after the Russian Revolution of October 1917. The Soviet Union broke up in 1991.

stronghold a strongly defended position.

Sword code name for one of the Normandy beaches captured by British troops during D-Day.

Tehran Conference the meeting of the Big Three Allied leaders — Roosevelt, Churchill, and Stalin — at Tehran, Iran, in November 1943. They set the place and time for D-Day.

U-boats German submarines of World War II.

unconditional no bargaining allowed.

Utah code name for one of the Normandy beaches taken by U.S. troops during D-Day. Utah was the westernmost of the invasion beaches and troops landing there suffered the fewest casualties.

Warsaw Pact a May 1955 treaty in which certain Eastern European countries entered into an alliance with the Soviet Union to give each other mutual military assistance in the event of an attack by NATO countries.

FURTHER INFORMATION

BOOKS

The Allied Victory. The World Wars (series).   Sean Sheehan (Raintree/Steck Vaughn)

The Attack on Pearl Harbor. Cornerstones of Freedom, Second Series (series).   Tom McGowen (Chirdren's Book Press)

Causes of World War II. Twentieth Century Perspectives (series). Paul Dowswell (Heinemann Library)

Hiroshima: The Shadow of the Bomb. Point of Impact (series).   Richard Tames (Heinemann Library)

Navajo Code Talkers.   Nathan Aaseng (Walker)

Pearl Harbor: The U.S. Enters World War II. Point of Impact (series).   Richard Tames (Heinemann Library)

The Tuskegee Airmen: African-American Pilots of World War II. Journey to Freedom — The African American Library (series).
Sarah E. De Capua (Childs World)

WEB SITES

www.army.mil/cmh-pg/books/wwii/7-8/7-8_1.htm
Learn about the pivotal Battle of the Bulge in the Ardennes.

www.usmint.gov/kids/coinNews/coinofthemonth/2004/11.cfn
Learn how Native American Code Talkers helped the Allies win the war.

americanhistory.si.edu/subs/historysubsbeforenuc/ww2/
Travel the oceans on WWII submarines.